Funny Spam Emails

by

Manley Peterson

To all those who need a laugh today

I just read that something like 200 billion spam emails are sent out to unsuspecting email addresses *every single day*. Now, I'm no math-magician, but I know that number is pretty big. To help you imagine it, just think of the number two, and then add eleven zeroes behind it. (Just joking, I know that doesn't help at all. Just know it is a crazy big number of spam emails...every single day.) But where do all these spam emails come from? Well, I'm sure some are composed by humans, some by computer programs, and probably some by aliens or chimpanzees. Who knows anymore?

The following pages are full of real spam emails that I have received. Spam, spam, and more of that delicious spam all over my inbox. Normal emails contain five fields: From, Date, Subject, To, and Body. To make things simpler to read in this book, I have omitted the Date and To fields from each email, since they are irrelevant.

When I started to read through these spam emails in my account, I was surprised to find a few that were genuinely funny, although I doubt that was the original intention. And, others were either annoying, sad, or downright creepy. Most of the following spam emails are full of contradictions, misspellings, and poor grammar. I think those mistakes kind of add a special flavor to the spam. Just for fun, I made up snide remarks and funny comebacks and wrote them below each email in italics. I figured other people would get a kick out of these silly and weird emails, too.

So, without further ado, please enjoy.

From: "Masanda Y" <masandayusufu@gmail.com>
Subject: Hello Dear

Hello my dearest,

I Blessed you with due respect in the name of God. Firstly I thank you so much, I feel blessed for you to read my massage, I am more than happy to be the subject of your thought my friend. My favorite language is English and I speak English very fluently. Awaiting to hear from you soonest.

Yours,

Baker

Dearest Masanda/Baker, I feel truly blessed to receive your email. And super-dee-duper blessed to read about your "massage." It felt great to know you were happy because I had one thought about you at some point in my life. By the way, you speak the English so well and fluently. Very soonest, you will hear from me, Baker. Goodbye, dear.

From: Nicole Watson <bemo@sighthelp.nett>
Subject: Hey! I am so lucky to find you.

Hey handsome! How are you doing today? My name is Nicole. I am 22 years old . I got your email from one of the mutual friends in facebook. I think you're cute and very brutal, I like that kind of guys.

I just looking to know you more, maybe start with whatsApp ?

please don't let me without answer

Nicole, no! I am so lucky to have found you! So, you like brutal guys, eh? Well, I am what some would call "very brutal" but also gentle and kind. But mostly brutal. And I would never "let you without answer," okay? Never. I think that makes perfect sense for us to start using whatsApp, since we only have facebook and email to communicate through. I think using all three programs at the same time shows a certain kind of intelligence.

From: Irina <linda@currencyimprovise.com>
Subject: Why are you sending me this?

Hey YOU, Please stop sending me your
pictures. :) Thanks.

*Who? ME? Oh, sorry about sending you all
those pictures of coins and paper money. I didn't
realize that you (Irina/Linda) from Currency
Improvise didn't want my pictures. I'm truly sorry.
Please forgive me. :) Thanks.*

From: Laura Stein <Glori@geta.sparsefoliage.com>

Subject: RE : Why haven't you answered my texts ?

Hey ! if you don't want to talk to me, just say it. - Sent from my iPhone

Hey, Laura/Glori. Okay, I'll try to be clear here. I'm just going to come out and say it. I don't want to talk with you, okay? I hope that isn't too harsh, but I'm just not comfortable with your proclivity for sparse foliage. I require thicker clumps of plants all around me. You understand, right?

From: Maria <Dolores@bookspages.net>

Subject: Message on hold

Hey dude,

Do you want me to wire the money I owe you this week or the next one?

I've been trying to reach you - About your money.

Answer me ASAP

Goodbye.

Maria, dude, please take this message off hold now. I've been trying to reach YOU – about my money. Of course, I want my money back this week. Please wire it immediately. I'm answering you ASAP, as you can tell. Goodbye.

From: Robert <st8Ah@e0owebt.com>
Subject: =>Attn: Your Pending Payment

Hi, get started today!

Hope you are doing well. We were notified that you may be eligible for new career advancement grant. If you have not taken advantage of this program, the deadline is approaching soon!!

$5,703 can be direct deposited in your account, should you quality for the grant.

This is a grant from the Government. This does not have to be paid back.

Robert, this is so awesome. I was just thinking to myself that I should apply for a grant from the Government, but I wasn't sure if I could "quality" for it. I need the money to start my new mole rancher career, and $5,703 is exactly how much it costs for my leather chaps plus accessories. Thanks friend!

From: Jackson <safety@sighthelp.net>

Subject: 1 quastion

Hi

Could you love me 1 day ????

Oh, Jackson. What a whopper of a "quastion." I almost don't know what to say. That's like one of the sweetest things I've ever heard from someone I've never met. I'm just not sure if 1 day would be enough. It might be 2 days. Or 3 days. Heck, it might extend to 4 days. I have a lot of love to give.

From: Mary Moore <qlvsr4hbcqn@mx22.art.com>
Subject: hey i think i've found my soulmate

hey u, I just need to tell you that you looked very nice today.. how amazing was this day for me thank you (y) Sent from my iPhone

Hey Mary. I'm so glad you emailed me, because I was trying to get a hold of you and I guess I had your email address wrong. See, I was typing in "qlvsr5hbcqn" instead of "qlvsr4hbcqn" this whole time, so you can see my confusion. But anyway, woo-hoo, what a nice thing to say. I think we could be soulmates, too. I'm glad I made your day so amazing. But, you know, I was home all day. I didn't go anywhere, so which window in my house were you looking in? Was it the bathroom one, again?

From: Reina <dr@sighthelp.net>

Subject: Blocked?

Hey! did you block me on Whatsapp?! I am hurt.

Reina, please, forgive me. I never wanted to hurt you. No, I didn't block you on Whatsapp. I hope we can clear up this misunderstanding. Also, are you a doctor now? One of those "sight help" doctors that I hear so much about?

From: Hi <info@okadzik.top>

Subject: Re: .unsubscribe NOW

To STOP receiving these emails from us Just hit relpy and let us know Thanks,

Dear Hi. I <u>do</u> want to stop receiving your emails, but I cannot find that darn "relpy" button anywhere. Is it supposed to be next to the "forwrad" button or something?

From: The Shepherds Diet <info@assist.1and1.fr>

Subject: BibIes Hidden Fat LosS Secret REVEALED

If you're overweight and you've prayed to God for help, He may be answering you through this email.

Oh, my God. My prayers have been officially answered. Yes, I am overweight. And I have prayed to God to reveal the hidden fat loss secrets of the Bible for many weeks. I think it's so awesome that God joined the 21st century and started emailing his replies. But I guess I shouldn't be surprised. I mean, what deity doesn't use email nowadays? I heard from a friend that Zeus started to use Twitter now.

From: Sophia <team-b@sighthelp.net>

Subject: Let's have fun this week like the old days

Hey , Can we meet this weekend for a drink or more? (you know what I mean by more right?) Give me an answer NOW. Sincerely -CheckMate-

Sophia (or should I just call you CheckMate from now on?), I can absolutely meet you this weekend for a drink, or maybe more (wink, wink). I think I know exactly what you mean. You want to borrow my pink spandex pants again, don't you? You devil! It'll be just like we used to do in the old days.

From: Contact <c-williams@simorbit.com>

Subject: (1) Message is waiting for you

Hellooo!

Long time no see. Where are you hiding? Wanna grab a drink tonight?

I think I am an alcoholic now haha

TEXT ME AFTER YOU READ THIS

See you

Hey Contact. Yes, long time, no see. You still working for SimOrbit? I was hiding today in the janitor's closet. Didn't you hear me knocking on the door for help? I was all tangled up in the mop bucket handle and almost died, haha. I'm glad you think you're an alcoholic now. I think that's just great. And, now that I've read this email, I'll close this program, and open up my texting program just to respond to your email. Such efficiency! See you.

From: The Google <notification@discovertort.com>
Subject: Your account will be deactivated

This is to inform you that your request to remove your account from gmail.com server has been approved and will initiate in one hour from the exact time you open this message.

Regards. ignore this message to continue with email removal or If this deactivation was not requested by you Please reply us.

Regards,

Google

Regards right back at you, The Google. I really do <u>not</u> want you to remove my account from the gmail.com server in exactly one hour from now, so that's why I'm responding right now. I think I've got like 53 minutes left. Also, I'm intrigued about the tort you discovered. Regards, The Google, a thousand times, regards.

From: Diana22 <3VS07djjj52C3.go.work-hard.org>

Subject: I sent you my new naked pics

HI,-I m only 2.3 miles away

academia.edu

Hi Diana22. What happened to Diana21? Oh no, did she work too hard at Work-Hard and blow out her positronic circuits? Did they have to melt her down and start over? I guess, in a way, Diana22, you are Diana21's offspring. I cannot believe you are only 2.3 miles away right now. That's awesome. What a coincidence. I'm only about 2.3 miles from you, too. I'm at the academia building, so come on over and say hello. And make sure you bring your new naked mole rat pics.

From: Anastasia Single <info@k8unsuitable.com>
Subject: WHAT VERY MAN DREAMS oF.

SEE FOR YOURSELF THAT ANASTASIA HAS EVERYTHING YOURE LOOKING FOR IN A WOMAN THE BEST, THE BRIGHTEST, THE MOST SENSUAL AND MOST INTOXICATINGLY BEAUTIFUL WOMEN ON EARTH.

Anastasia Single. The name just rolls off my tongue like chunky peanut butter. And I'm a man. A "very" man. I hear Anastasia is the best, the brightest, and most intoxicating of all women on earth. That's no small feat. But I think I'll pass for now. I think I can do better than the best. It's what I dream of.

From: Force Factor <info@k8unsuitable.com>

Subject: New Testosterone Booster Hits the Shelves

Are you ready to build a ripped athletic body? LEGENDARY PERFORMANCE STARTS HERE, Try it FREE Today

Dear Force Factor, I have been ready for many days to build a ripped athletic body. That's why I've been grave robbing in the city cemeteries. Please don't tell anybody about my crimes, especially the guys over at "k8unsuitable.com" who might think I'm unsuitable to continue in my job as a daycare provider for the baby Igors of the world.

From: Mia <4671S17MS17MJ@4671j.sighthelp.net>
Subject: I Need Your Answer Now !!

Hello, I have a party this weekend at home. It's gonna be crazy though. I am waiting for your answer. You do not wanna miss it.

Mia, hey girl, what's up? So, you're finally gonna have that party you've been talking about. Awesome! I'll be there, but only if you promise it's going to be so much crazier than your last baby shower. I didn't think it was possible to stuff that many babies into your shower, but you proved me wrong. Let's see if you can top it this time. I'm in!

From: Friedrich And Ann Mayrho <info@ufrnet.br>
Subject: Donation For Charity Work

Good Day,

My wife and I have awarded you with a donation of $ 1,000,000.00 Dollars from part of our Jackpot Lottery of 50 Million Dollars, respond with your details for claims.

We await your earliest response and God Bless you.

Friedrich And Ann Mayrho.

Hi Friedrich And Ann. So, it was you who won that Jackpot Lottery for 50 Million Dollars, huh? I'm so happy for you both. And, I'm honored to be recognized for my charity work. It took a long time for me to remove all that gum from the urinals in Yankee Stadium. $1,000,000 seems okay, I guess. A little lower than I was hoping to get, but I'll take it. Thanks again.

From: Angela <angela007@flagfonderie.com>
Subject: attention

Hi,

I know your name and you live near me . Are you interested to know your future? I may surprise you and give courage and strength that you need.Would like to have answers about what you want. Love Money Luck This is not a joke! You have only until today to try it.

Phew! I'm glad this is not a joke. I know your name, too. You are Angela. And you live near me, right? I think I do need love, money, and luck. Please surprise me. However, since you put me on such a tight deadline, I will have to reschedule my mom and dad's funeral today. They both jumped out of an airplane last week for their 50th wedding anniversary. Oh, don't worry, they landed safely, but then immediately got ran over by a bus.

From: Huan <HuanHuan@farrand.plxqtcgjh72.fr>
Subject: Angel Or Naughty I'm Whatever You Want.

Hey,

How long haven't you felt a butterfly in your stomach? Who knows where a simple "Hi" might take you..

You know what, HuanHuan? It <u>has</u> been a while since I've felt a butterfly in my stomach. Probably back in grade school when I swallowed one alive to see if it would tickle me from the inside. Anyway, I'm intrigued about your offer for a simple "Hi," but I'm also shy and worried where it might take me. But, on the other hand, if that simple "Hi" takes me to Lambeau Field to watch the Packers play, I'm willing to give it a chance. So, let me know.

From: Steve Dillon <col.steve@adagio.ocn.ne.jp>
Subject: I HAVE A BUSINESS PROPOSAL

I am Steve Dillon, a U.S soldier. I came across your email when I was searching for a random person online who I can trust with this proposal. I am willing to offer you 40% of the total money which is $9.8 million USD if you are willing to do the deal with me and I also want you to know that this is very legit.

you can reply me here if you are willing to do this deal with me and I will advise you ahead on how I will send the funds out to you. I will wait for your response.

Hi, Steve. I like the cut of your jib. You take chances. I admire that. I like your style. In fact, the next time I need major surgery, I will search online for a random person I can trust to operate on me. And, believe you me, that is very legit.

From: George Brennan <kaupe-zi@pure.ocn.ne.jp>
Subject: Re:Compliments.

Compliments,

This is to inform you that your consignment Box is still in our custody and we are ready to serve you better. This package was abandoned here by some delivery agent from AFRICA long ago. I am currently in charge and I shall be waiting to hear back from you.

Best Regards,

George Brennan

Inspection Officer Storage Department.

Compliments to you, too, George. My, you look nice today. One of the best-looking members of the Inspection Officer Storage Dept. I've ever seen. I don't recall which delivery agent from AFRICA that might have been, since I work with so many. I'll call AFRICA right now and find out.

From: Rev. Dr. John Wool <westernunion@ne.jp>
Subject: Attention:

Attention:

This is to inform you that the America Embassy office was instructed to transfer your fund $10 million dollars U.S Dollars compensating all the SCAM VICTIMS and your email was found as one of the VICTIMS. Furthermore you are advised to call us as the instruction was passed that within 6hours without hearing from you, Count your paymentcanceled.

Thanks Rev. Dr. John Wool,

Dearest Reverend Doctor John Wool from Western Union of Japan. Can I just call you R.D.J.W.W.U.J for short? I absolutely want my $10 million dollars in US Dollars, as compensation for being a SCAM VICTIM. I hope I made it under the 6-hour deadline. Please get back to me soon, sir.

From: Mr Robert Brown <www@fine.ocn.ne.jp>
Subject: I am Mr Robert Brown

I am Mr Robert Brown The Delivery Agent and I am written to inform you about your Bank Cheque Draft brought by the United Embassy from the government of Benin Republic in the white house Washington DC I will like you to reconfirm to me the following details: Your phone number, Your current home address, Your full name, Occupation, Nearest Airport, I'D copy.

Yours Sincerely,

Mr Robert Brown.

Sorry, I didn't catch your name. Anyway, I <u>am</u> willing to reconfirm my info to get that "cheque draft" under one condition. I am willing to provide my full name, home address, SSN, DOB, bank account, and routing numbers. But I'll be damned if I'll reveal the nearest airport to me. Good day, sir!

From: Newsletter Nofitication <q462@q6t.re.com>
Subject: Incomplete information, Please respond!

Hi

My name is Marton Pholock, The creator of email newsletters! Last week i found your email registered in some of my newsletter but with missing the following info : First Name & Zip Code, would you kindly try to re-fill these info! Looking forward to hearing from you! Thank You Marton

Marton Pholock, you are a legend around these parts. I cannot believe I'm actually conversing with the "creator of email newsletters." I mean, you are essentially a god in the world of computing computers and digital delivery of important information from Nigeria. Sorry about my incomplete personal information. I'll get it to you soon. I appreciate the newsletter "nofitication."

From: James Fisher <Sir@mountain.ocn.ne.jp>
Subject: YOUR URGENT REPLY IS NEEDED.

This notice is been directed to you because your email address was found in one of the scam Artists file and computer hard-disk while the investigation, maybe you have been scammed. You are therefore being compensated with sum of ($10.7 Million) US Dollars valid into an ATM Card.

We advice you to stop all the communications with everyone regarding your payment as we have short listed to deliver to you and now urge you to comply and receive your ATM Card funds.

Holy crap, you found my email address in the "scam Artists file" during an investigation? Do not worry! I will comply with you. I will stop all communications with everyone, including my only daughter, who is having a belly button transplant surgery today. Now send me the money!

From: Jessica <IRdOit@studioserver.com.br>

Subject: Are YOU??? ..

Hi, We Need To Talk

--Sent from my iphone

Jessica, sweet Jessica. I need to talk right now, too. If only you had one of those new-fangled talking devices that are all the rage nowadays, then we could keep it real. P.S. Do You Like Capital Letters? –Sent from my ear-phone

From: Maria <YSDZ8C@chrdvh.webviclati.com>

Subject: Hello,are you still single?

Hello,

Do you remember me ? I m Maria,25 yo We changed messages last year on facebook. Are you still single man? Can we meet ? I have some new photos for you,I m on-line now. Waiting for your reply

Kisses

Maria

Hey Maria. No, sorry, I'm not single anymore. I kind of remember you, but my memory is a little fuzzy, probably because we "changed the messages" too many times on facebook. Were you the lady that used to eat superglue in YouTube videos? Or that other lady who liked to jump into swimming pools wearing dime-store reptile costumes?

From: SkypeNotify <elloco@brasilnet.net>

Subject: You have missed mails on Skype

Skype

You have missed mail

2 mails

Sincerely yours

SkypeNotify

Dear SkypeNotify. Isn't that the strangest coincidence we have such similar names? I'm Skype. You're SkypeNotify. LOL, it's like we were destined to meet. Hey, maybe we are related? Was your dad's name SkypeSenior, by any chance? Anyway, thank you so much for letting me know about my missed mail, or more specifically, my 2 mails. I will try to keep on top of these things better. I appreciate the shout-out.

From: List Owner <be.ebstch475@8u.w1.reajrd.tk>
Subject: Is Your Husband GettingCalls Day n Night?

Strange Numbers, Late Night Texts? Cheaters Hate This Site. SEE WHO THEY CALLING & TEXTING.

Enter The Number, Uncover the TRUTH.

Curses, it's true. My husband has been getting calls "Day n Night." And I think they were from Strange Numbers. Heaven help me, what do I do? Oh, List Owner, you are my only hope at this point. Should I just leave without saying goodbye or file for divorce from the back of a cab? Please get back to me ASAP. I'm trying to stay rational, but I need to uncover the TRUTH.

From: Ms. Rose Kelly <jpmcb@lime.ocn.ne.jp>

Subject: Greetings

Hello my dear,

In accordance to my religious persuasion, I felt expedient to inform you on the wicked conspiracy hatched by the Ministry Of Finance to divert your funds to their designated account in Cayman Island but unfortunately, they now moved the funds down to Africa and hide it in a security company in other to buy time. Please do not expose my person, it is not easy to get employment around here and I cannot contend with these powerful individuals because they can eliminate me.

I cannot believe my funds are hidden in Africa. Damn that Ministry Of Finance! Bless you Rose Kelly and your religious persuasion. Hear me now, I promise never to expose your person and accidentally contribute to your elimination.

From: Mr. Watkins Joseph <ac@southplastic.com>
Subject: Urgent Attention......

    The United States Department of Treasury has retrieved all Files of illegal transactions and we will be working under a legitimate arrangement to ensure that you follow the normal process to receive your fund (AMOUNT: $6.500,00000 USD).

    call or text me on the phone number for anything you do not understand

    Regard

    Mr. Joseph Watkins

    United States Special investigator

Jumping Jehoshaphat, Joseph. Boy am I glad you contacted me. Look at all those zeroes after that decimal. I cannot believe I'm entitled to receive exactly six and a half dollars, assuming we can follow the normal process to receive my funds. US Department of Treasury bringing the heat. Regard.

From: BRIAN GORDON <Lap5@guitar.ocn.ne.jp>
Subject: Claim your abandon fund.

Please do forgive me for taking much of your time for going through this mail which you will conclude by saying that it is just a common thing to you every-day if am not mistaken, we knew that at least you have encounters numbers of similar mails like this before, but please do not mistake that everybody who reach you are all scammers or either a fraudster as well. Anyway my name is Mr. Brian Gordon from Nigeria, i am currently to help you claim your abandon fund of a scam victims of $500,000 that was stored in a bank here in USA California. Reconfirm your details, Also Call me

Brian Gordon, the man with two first names. Look, don't worry, I <u>do</u> forgive you for taking much of my time for going through this mail, which I will conclude by saying it is a common thing. Peace out.

From: INFO <3slY3CSKgi@3sly35jicskgi.rose.com>
Subject: Re,WORK WITH US

We would like you to work with us, as our company is expanding Canada and the USA, and we would like you to act as our Payment Receiving Officer (PRO) in your region for more information please reply to this MSG.

Oh, INFO, this sounds like a game changer. Your company is able to expand both Canada <u>and</u> the USA? That is crazy. I mean, I heard it might be possible (through science!) to make Canada slightly bigger by sticking a large tube into the ground and pumping questionable gases into the earth's mantle, but never in my wildest dreams did I think you could pull that off in the USA, too. Your company sounds amazing. Sign me up. I will be your PRO.

From: Capt. Kate Carr <dsgloviH@poem.ocn.ne.jp>
Subject: PERSONAL MESSAGE....

I know you will be surprised to read my email.
Apart from being surprise you may be skeptical to
reply me, because a lot of scammers are out there.
My name is Captain Kate Carr. I discovered 2 trunk
boxes containing American dollar. Am looking for a
trust worthy individual who will assist me to receive
the funds in his country before i will come over and
join the person

Best Regards, Capt. Kate Carr

*Captain Kate, you scared me. Honestly, I
almost dropped the baby I was holding, because I
was so surprised (but not skeptical!) by your email.
Whose baby? I am not sure. In any event, I am a
trustworthy individual and would be willing to
assist you to bring over to the US that one dollar
you found. I do not think that will be very hard.*

From: American Embassy <www@peace.ocn.ne.jp>
Subject: American Embassy

United Bank For African, has come to agreement to send your funds in consignment worth about $7.5 Million Usd without any further delay and they have did as instructed by the United Nation, as matter of fact your funds has already arrived in the one of the airports in your country but the diplomat signaled us that he lost your contact address. I advice you urgently now to reconfirm you're your information, So that can deliver your fund as soon as possible.

Finally, after all this time, the United Bank for African is sending my money. I mean, the whole reason that bank exists is because of me (I'm the one African). Let's just take out the middle man. I'll drive around the country and search all the airports myself. That should not take too long.

From: MR. TONY WILLIAMS <la@lagames.com>
Subject: Attention: My Dear Friend,

How are you, hope you are fine? This message is coming to you from WESTERN UNION BOARD OF DIRECTORS In order to PROOF the legitimacy of this transaction, we decided to issue your first installation payment of $2,500.00 as an evidence to show that this transaction is real, genuine and 100% percent risk free, but you can not pick up the payment because it's (ON-HOLD) and it needs to be RE-ACTIVATED before you can be able to pick up. and the activation fee will only cost you the sum of $155.00

Tony Jabrony, my dear friend, I am doing great, thanks. Okay, so you only need a $155 fee from me to "re-activate" the "on-hold" transaction that you started and purposely put on-hold? I guess that makes sense, so I will send it soon.

From: Congratulations <Gf320Z2@prodles.com>
Subject: You may have received a SAM'S reward

HI, Your Order no #812-4623 might have ARRIVED Will you be the next Lucky Recipient? Crack the Egg!!
   Sam's Club
   Reward Inside!
   Crack

Well, based upon the contents of this email, it is obvious to me that <u>crack</u> is involved. I "may have" received a reward? My order "might have" ARRIVED? Well, don't leave me sitting on pins and needles, Congratulations, spit it out. Did I get anything or not? Give me my Reward! (Oh no, don't tell me it's crack!?!)

From: Mr. Allen Large <iii-x21@vir-g0r-5k.gq>
Subject: YOUR DONATION GIFT

I hope this information meet you well as I know you will be curious to know why/how I selected you to receive a cash sum of $2,000,000 USD, our information below is 100% legitimate, We searched over the internet for assistance because i saw your profile on Microsoft email owners list and picked you..

I am hoping that you will be able to use the money wisely and judiciously over there in your country.

God bless you, Allen and Violet Large

Hi, Mr. and Mrs. Large. I hope you will agree my reply is 100% legitimate. I searched all over the internet for assistance on how to accept your cash, but I could not find your profile on the Microsoft email owners list, so I am a failure and not worthy.

From: Mr. William C. Dudley <ww@bell.ocn.ne.jp>
Subject: Federal Reserve Bank

Did you authorize Mrs. Annette Stillman of Kemuning Ray Street NO.8,Tomang. Jakarta, Indonesia to pay the pending wire transfer charges and claim your WORLD BANK/IMF assisted scam victim compensation funds of $9.5millonUSD?

She is here with us now. YOU ARE ALERTED TO REPLY SO URGENT NOW ! NOW !

Sincerely.

Mr. William C. Dudley

Director Federal Reserve Bank

Bill, I don't think you are taking this SERIOUSLY ENOUGH! I do not know that lady at all. Don't let her take my money. Don't let her escape. Call the police, call the army, for the love of God, do something. P.S., may I call you Duddy? I think that would be a cute nickname for you.

From: Diplomat Michael Krop <dip.office@jas.jp>
Subject: I' AM Diplomat Michael Krop

I hope you are very fine?

Please I want to let you know that I am on my way to your house to deliver your $ 2.5 million dollars, which was recovered by the United State Embassy in Benin Republic, so I want to ensure that I complete the delivery of the fund to you today. Honestly I really need to ensure I complete the delivery of the fund to you. Await your feedback right away.

Warmest Regard

Diplomat Michael Krop

Hey Mike, did you ever get that diplomat job? It isn't clear in the email. Anyway, yes, I am fine, but I am not home right now, so just leave the money in my front yard by the dog. Honestly, I need you to do that to ensure complete delivery.

From: Mr.Amancio Ortega <Tpga@aros.ocn.ne.jp>
Subject: You have been gifted With Some Funds

You have been gifted $2 MILLION USD in 2017 Donation Funds. Use the money wisely, this is the only thing that makes my wife happy too even now that she is not here with me anymore, we have too much to give away as I only have a few months left on earth. Thank you for accepting our offer, we are indeed grateful You Can Google my name for more information: Mr.Amancio Ortega.

God bless you

Mr.Amancio Ortega world's 4th-richest man Billionaire investor.

Mr. Ortega, are you an alien (maybe ALF)? Your wife already left for your home planet, didn't she? You are probably lonely. I will take the funds, but I'm a little disappointed in your ranking. I usually only take monetary gifts from the top three.

From: Victoria Dates <Absolute.v45@6.enzcjr.cf>
Subject: Girls battle for your heart: choose
Aleksandra or Nilla

The ONLY site that gets you a girl!

WARNING! There are LOTS of gorgeous
women on this site. Please be discreet. Only for 30+

*I can't believe it! There are literally girls
battling for my heart? That's super cool. I'm
completely flattered. Oh, but don't worry. I'll be
very discreet. But who to choose? Aleksandra
sounds nice. On the other hand, Nilla must be
wonderful, too. Well, I guess I'll just wait until the
battle is over and see who is still alive.*

From: Sarah <KQIQRA@jtk.cnn.com>

Subject: Over 18!

THIS IS IMPORTANT ARE YOU OVER 18! REPLY ASAP!

Dear Sarah, yes, I can see how important this email is by your gratuitous use of capital letters. So, emphatically, I will answer you. YES, yes, yes, I am over 18! Thanks for asking. Oh, crap, is this is an undercover operation from a CNN reporter?

From: CustomTobacco <edward.ctbc41043@ju.ga>
Subject: Holiday Cigars at Great Prices!

40% OFF PERSONALIZED CIGARS

Personailzed cigars are the perfect gift for any occasion. Add a name, a photo, or a special note on your fully customized cigar band to make our premium cigars your own! Get Started!

Yes, let's get started! Nothing says Happy Holidays like giving out cancer sticks as a gift. And at 40% off, no less. Hmm, what should I put on the personalized cigar? A note that says, "Hope you enjoy this cigar. Now smoke it for your chance to have lifelong breathing problems and ultimately die a slow, horrible death. Love you."

From: Heart Health <noreply@oyeinboxmail.com>
Subject: 4 Heart Attack Warnings You Shouldn't Ignore.

1 in 3 people die from Heart Disease... SO, unfortunately, there is a very good chance YOU will die from a heart attack or heart disease.

Oh, thanks a lot, Heart Health. Way to start my day. I thought I'd check my email in the morning and get started on the right foot, but no! You had to come along and basically guarantee I'll be dying soon. By the way, there is a better than 1 in 3 chance I'll be deleting your email within the next few seconds.

From: MONEY GRAM <afiq@strateqgrp.com>

Subject: WE HAVE SENT YOUR $5,000USD

ATTENTION DEAR, PLEASE READ THIS MESSAGE VERY CAREFUL AND FOLLOW THE INSTRUCTION

I have sent you several notices concerning the claim of your benefit that was paid to you as compensation from Benin Republic following my petition against the Government since 2015 as the a human right activist to compensate you with the sum of $15,000.00 USD This amount will be made available again within 20 minutes after you have settled the activation fee $70 USD

Money Gram, dear, I don't think this is worth it. Only $15,000? You gotta do better than that. I get emails every day for millions and billions, so you gotta bring your "A" game next time. PLEASE FOLLOW MY INSTRUCTION.

From: Mr. Ming Mui <MuiM@aioros.ocn.ne.jp>
Subject: I will be waiting to hear from you

Dear Friend,

Seeing this email message would be a surprise to you . However, this correspondence is UN-official and private, and it should be treated as such. I also guarantee you that this transaction is hitch free from all what you may think of. Late Mr. Wiiliam Aucoin was an account holder in my branch; he owns a dollar account with a sum of money deposited in a Secret account with my branch. After the transfer of the money to your nominated bank account, we shall share the money 70-30.that is I will have 70% while you will have 30%.

Truly, Ming Mui, bank of China (USA).

Mr. Mui (Bank of China USA using Japanese email account), yes, I agree let's split that dollar 70/30. I'll take my 30 cents in pesos, please.

From: Victoria <victoria@rmjygtmki31.fr>
Subject: I love your profile, let's meet us in

Hey, I know you live near me at. I want to meet you if you're still interested by me?

You can check my pictures there if you forgot me :'(

I wait your news!

Victoria

Victoria, "let's meet us in" where exactly? I just checked your profile, and you are hiding your address as well as every other identifying characteristic. Also, your pictures only show stock images of potato salad. So, I've been wracking my brain trying to remember you, but alas, you must be easily forgettable. Sorry to make you "wait your news!"

From: Thank You <vswB@je612.vz2ihq.cisco.com>

Subject: Are you ?

Why did you block me!!

Dear Thank You, yes, I did block you. Thank you for asking, Thank You. Godspeed.

From: US Special investigator <3hr54w@noild.jp>
Subject: HAVE YOU BEEN ABLE TO?

HAVE YOU BEEN ABLE TO RECEIVE YOUR FUNDS? I 'm contacting you by your email however, I feel it's best and more convenient for me to explain why I am contacting you. I'm Mr. Patrick Morrisey a United States Special investigator, For your information, it was truly confirmed that you have 100% Legitimate unpaid transaction and you have every right to claim this funds as you're been confirmed to be the right Beneficiary of the said amount $5.5 Million usd Hit reply and confirm.

Regard

Mr. Patrick Morrisey, US Special investigator

Patrick, US Investigator from Japan, thank you for following up with me. No, I haven't received my 100% legitimate unpaid funds yet. Are you sure you "truly confirmed" them for me?

From: Miss. Elizabeth Nelson <www@tiara.c.ne.jp>
Subject: Dear beloved,

My dear i believe that you have not forgotten me, although it was indeed a very long time we communicate last. Well, this is to thank you for your past effort to assist me in moving out my late Father's funds out the country a that time, I understand your thought that time, that I wasn't for real and you said that I am a scam but I told you that am not a scam and you understood me. Now i want you to contact our parish priest: Reverend Father Enoch William who used to be a good father to me when I was in UN refugee Camp in Cotonou, Republic of Beninf (US$2,000,000.00) Two million United State dollars, which I prepared for you and kept for your compensation for all efforts. Good bye for now

I'm speechless. You lost me at "Dear beloved."

From: Tawanda <TawandaMaranto@acticites.com>

Subject: Please confirm your unclaimed assets

Dear,

You may have unclaimed assets! We have found this we matched it to you. To claim your assets, please reply here

We retrieved these information *actually*:

First Name

Last Name

Email address

City

Thank you,

Tawanda MoneyFinder

Unclaimed assets! So cool. Oh, Tawanda MoneyFinder, you have outdone yourself. I have verified you have all my information correct (actually!) in your email, so I'll just wait here for my money.

From: Your partner <WB6QF5@chrdh.wbati.com>
Subject: New message

I really bilieve that you are the greatest thing to ever happen to me.

Wow, I truly "bilieve" that, too, partner. And I'm not just saying that to be nice. Truly. The. Greatest. Thing. To. Ever. Happen. To. Me. Period.

From: Ur Ex <K2JrJ4FDn@kfdn.primeirrose.com>
Subject: Im warning youuu !!!!!!!!

Hi You , Stop f** calling me ----
Motherf***er!!!?!
Sent from my iPhone

Hi, Ur Ex, I'm sensing some hostility here. I mean, I appreciate your friendly "Hi" to begin the conversation, but it quickly devolves into meanness and scariness. I figure once the words with asterisks come out, things can only get worse. So, I'll take your warning and skedaddle.

Author's Note

Well, I hope you enjoyed the absurdity of some of these spam emails. I know I'm not the only one to receive these, so maybe this book will pique your interest enough to open up that dusty spam folder in your email account and see if you can spot any hidden gems. But be careful...the spam never stops.

You can discover more of my books on Amazon. Please leave a review to let me know your thoughts.

Manley Peterson
December 2017

manleypeterson.com

www.ingramcontent.com/pod-product-compliance
Lightning Source LLC
La Vergne TN
LVHW092354060326
832902LV00008B/1023